Twas the First Christmas Eve

Written by
Lisa Bruce

Illustrated by
Robert Bruce

Twas the First Christmas Eve

Copyright © 2019 Blue Oink Books

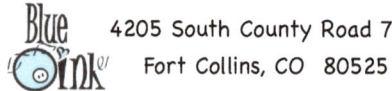 4205 South County Road 7
Fort Collins, CO 80525

All rights reserved.
No part of this book may be reproduced without express written permission from the author or illustrator.

Written by Lisa Bruce
Illustrated by Robert Bruce

ISBN: 9781734332100

To all children,
And to all who have the heart of a child,
There's a special place just for you near the manger.

Come and see!

'Twas the first Christmas Eve, and all through Israel's house,
The only room to be found was a cave shared by cows.

So Mary and Joseph prepared a place for their child,
In an old wooden manger, where some hay had been piled.

The stars held their breath,
And the winds became still,

When Jesus was born
In that cave on that hill.

Now in Bethlehem proper, in the middle of town,
People were streaming from lands all around.
They came for a census, not for vacation.
Like sheep they were counted, the whole Jewish nation!

For the Romans who occupied the land of the Jews,
Made them pay taxes, and obey all their rules.
God's Chosen People were forlorn and dismayed,
But they continued to hope, and oh how they prayed!

And they dreamt of being saved by a Savior so strong!
Yes that vision had danced in their heads for so long!

For so long they had waited for the Savior of lore.

They waited...

And waited...

Then they waited some more!

And they followed the rules of the Torah with care,
In hopes the Messiah soon would be there.

Now at last he had come!
He'd come from Heaven afar!
But did anyone notice the Savior's bright star?

I'm afraid most folks didn't. They were too busy being busy.
So busy, in fact, that they made themselves dizzy!
Shopping for doodads, for trinkets and treasures,
For gizmos and gadgets and tinselly pleasures.

But on the hillside adjacent to the bustling town,
A small band of shepherds had just settled down.
They were peaceful and calm, for they had no concern,
About what they should buy, or how much money they'd earn.

They simply gathered their sheep near a warm fire bright,
And prepared to keep watch through the long winter's night.

When suddenly, in the sky, there arose such a clatter,
They sprang to their feet to see what was the matter!
And what to their wondering eyes should appear,
But a flurry of feathers, amid shouts of "He's here!"

Yes a whole host of angels had rushed down from on high!
A whole host of angels praised God from the sky!

They sang and they clapped with their huge, mighty wings!
"Fear not," they announced, "Good tidings we bring!
For on this night the Savior is born unto you!
On this night your dream of a Savior's come true!"

And so the shepherds, so humble, were the first to behold,
And after them came three kings, bringing gifts, bringing gold!
The big burly shepherds all fell to their knees,
And the kings with their presents did likewise, all three!

Sweet little Jesus, so great yet so small,
Smiled a big smile at the sight of them all!
Oh His love was divine; it was perfect and pure!
There was no love like His love, of this they were sure!

And so goes the Christmas story, the one that you know.
And I bet you're now thinking, "I've heard all this before."
That's probably true, for the story's told often.
But there's one little something that's often forgotten.

One little detail, one twist to the plot,
That adds to the story. Yes it adds quite a lot!

The secret's no secret, for there's a way to discover,
A way to see for yourself, and a way to uncover,
The beautiful mystery hidden under the veil
Of this wondrous and wonderful TRUE Christmas tale.

Just open your hearts, yes open them wide,
And prepare to be shocked and amazed and surprised.
Then draw near to the manger, to our Savior and King,
Where His mother will tell you, "He wants only ONE thing."

"What thing?" you might ask.

Well here's one final clue:
The gift Jesus wants is spelled...

www.ingramcontent.com/pod-product-compliance
Lightning Source LLC
LaVergne TN
LVHW071028070426
835507LV00002B/67